TRACKING TIME IN ISRAEL

by Don McCluskey

Tracking Time
In Israel

by: Donald McCluskey

www.TheAppointedTimes.com

Rev. 0122216-01

Contents

Introduction – For Signs and for Seasons

How often have you marveled at the rising or setting sun as it set the sky ablaze with color? Have you ever beheld the beauty of a full or crescent moon and felt there must be some sort of meaning in this lesser light? These are some of the most common, yet magnificent events that bless our planet each day, and I am here to tell you that there is indeed some significance to be found these heavenly events.

I am certainly not suggesting astrology, but these lights and luminaries were placed in the heavens by the Creator to give light and to act as signs, so people could know the seasons, days, and years of our planet. These heavenly lights were created so mankind could know when to plant, harvest, conduct business, and even worship. In the account of creation, we read:

Then God said,
"Let there be lights in the expanse of the heavens to separate the day from the night, and let them be for signs, and for seasons, and for days and years;"

Genesis 1:14

One of the keys to interpreting the Scriptures is found in understanding how these lights were used by the ancient Israelites to track time. For example, when did a day begin and end? At what time of the year did the months of the Bible occur? What determined when a month began and ended? What is the meaning of twilight? What is a watch in the night? What is meant by the biblical references to hours, such as the third hour, the sixth hour, or ninth hour? These are excellent questions and knowing the answers can greatly enhance our understanding of God's Word.

Since precise time-measuring devices were not available in the ancient world, civilizations relied on observations of the sun, moon, and stars to track time. Our modern days end and begin at midnight, which is a point in the nighttime that can be precisely known only with the aid of an electronic or mechanical clock. But since ancient civilizations, including the nation of Israel, did not have such devices, they used the setting of the sun as their indicator of a new day.

The Israelites also tracked their months in a very different way than we do with our modern calendar. The Hebrew months are determined by observing the phases of the moon. Their months begin when the fine edge of the crescent new moon is first observed. From that date, the days are counted from sunset to sunset until the next crescent new moon is observed. Since the Hebrew calendar relies on both the moon and the sun, it is called a lunisolar calendar.

Since tracking time involves much more than a knowledge of days and months, we have created this reference guide, which contains the details of ancient Israel's calendaring system in concise form to assist you in understanding the message of God's Word.

The Hebrew Calendar

The calendar that was used by the ancient Israelites, also known as the Hebrew calendar, is still in use today in Jewish and Messianic circles. The details of this calendar are relatively easy to learn – many Jewish people learned it when they were children. It is fun and interesting and you can enjoy the pleasure of moon-watching while gaining an awareness of when significant days and events of the Bible begin and end.

Once again, I must emphasize that this is a study of astronomy—it is not astrology. Astrology is a form of divination, seeking hidden knowledge from sources other than God, such as spirits, speaking with the dead, and idol worship, all of which are abominations to God.[1] Astronomy is, among other things, the study of the heavenly bodies and how God set them in beautiful, predictable motion that we can use to track time. He declared that the lights of the heavens, the sun, moon, and the stars, were created for giving light, for signs, seasons, days, and years,[2] so it is perfectly acceptable for us to observe the lights of the heavens for this purpose.

In this reference guide, we will explore the ancient Hebrew concepts of

Day
Daytime
Nighttime
Twilight
Week
Sabbath
High Sabbath
Month
New Moon
Year

---

1   Isaiah 47:13 "Let now the astrologers, those who prophesy by the stars, those who predict by the new moons, stand up and save you from what will come upon you."

2   Genesis 1:14–18

The Appointed Times

Every student of the Bible would benefit by becoming familiar with the Appointed Times, also known as the Jewish holy days, which are recorded in chronological order in the 23rd chapter of Leviticus. We frequently refer to the Appointed Times in this guide since they provide many examples of timing in the Bible, but of greater importance, these special days reveal profound insights about the person and work of the Messiah.[3]

Day

The Hebrew day **begins** at sundown

God called the light day, and the darkness He called night. And there was evening and there was morning, one day.

Genesis 1:5

You might think it strange that the day would begin when the sun goes down; perhaps it would be easier to think of the day ending at sundown. Either way, the end of a day and the beginning of the next day occur simultaneously, at the same instant in time. It is important, however, to make sure that everyone in the community agrees about when the change-of-day occurs. Since digital and mechanical clocks did not exist during the time of Moses, the sunset was used as the indicator of the change of day.

---

3   *If you would like to learn more about the Appointed Times, I enthusiastically refer you to our book, The Messiah Beyond a Shadow of Doubt, which explores how the Appointed Times are shadows of things to come, but their substance is actually about the Messiah.*

Why did the Israelites choose sundown instead of sunrise? It was because of the wording in Genesis 1:5 (see above). Notice that evening was mentioned first, and then morning. Thus, the ancient Israelites considered a day to be from sunset to sunset. When the sun set, both the day and the date changed. This concept will be of great importance when you study Passover, since the lamb was killed on the afternoon of the 14th, and it was eaten after the sun had set. It would have been the same day from our modern perspective, but for the Israelites it was the next day, since the date changed to the 15th when the sun set.

This little piece of information is able to shed light on other Bible passages and increase your overall understanding of the Scriptures. For example, you may be familiar with the following account in the life of Jesus:

> *And when evening had come, **after the sun had set**,*
> *they began bringing to Him all who were*
> *ill and those who were demon-possessed.*
>
> Mark 1:32 (Emphasis added)

The paragraph that precedes this verse makes it clear that it was the Sabbath day (before the sun had set), which meant that the people were not allowed to do any labor, such as walking long distances or carrying heavy loads, including carrying their sick loved ones. But this verse explicitly says, "when evening had come, after the sun had set," which ushered in the next day. Suddenly, it was Sunday, the first day of the week, even though it would seem like Saturday night to you and me. The Sabbath Day had ended, along with its restrictions against work, so the people were allowed to walk long distances and bring their sick friends and loved-ones to Jesus.

By knowing the Hebrew time-keeping methods, we understand that the people were waiting for the sun to set. It was like watching the clock — they were watching the sun as it set, anticipating the moment they could take their sick to Jesus. They did not have to wait for midnight for the Sabbath to end – they went to Jesus immediately after the sun had set.

Caveat

I must mention one caveat within the naming convention that can mislead readers. Even though the calendar day begins at sundown, the evening portion of a day was sometimes referred to with the same date as the daytime.

For example, in Exodus 12:18, the Passover lamb was killed in the afternoon of Abib 14, but the evening of the same day is referred to as "the fourteenth day of the month at evening." This can be confusing since the calendar date had actually changed to Abib 15 at sundown. The same type of date reference can be seen regarding the Day of Atonement in Leviticus 23:32, which says, "on the ninth of the month at evening, from evening until evening you shall keep your sabbath." In reality, the date had changed to Tishri 10 at sundown, but the evening is referred to as the evening of the ninth. For the most part, however, the Scriptures are consistent about the day and date changing at sundown.

The Days are Numbered

As you read the Bible, you will notice that the Hebrew days do not have names such as Sunday, Monday, or Tuesday. Instead, they use ordinals (i.e. numbers or ordered items) to refer to their days, such as "the first day of the week," "the second day of the week," and so on. The counting begins with Sunday, which is the first day of the week. The only day that was named is the Sabbath Day, which is the seventh day. For ease of understanding, however, we will in most cases, use our familiar names of weekdays.[4]

---

4   *The names of the weekdays vary widely from country to country. In this guide, however, we will use the more common names: Sunday, Monday, Tuesday, Wednesday, Thursday, Friday, and Saturday.*

Daytime

In our modern world, the day is divided evenly into 24 hours. But in the ancient world, the daytime or *daylight* was divided into **twelve equal parts**, beginning at sunrise and ending at sundown. The twelve parts were called hours, and were called by their ordinal names, such as the first hour, the second hour, and so on.

Daytime was divided into twelve equal parts, beginning at sunrise and ending at sundown.

Daytime

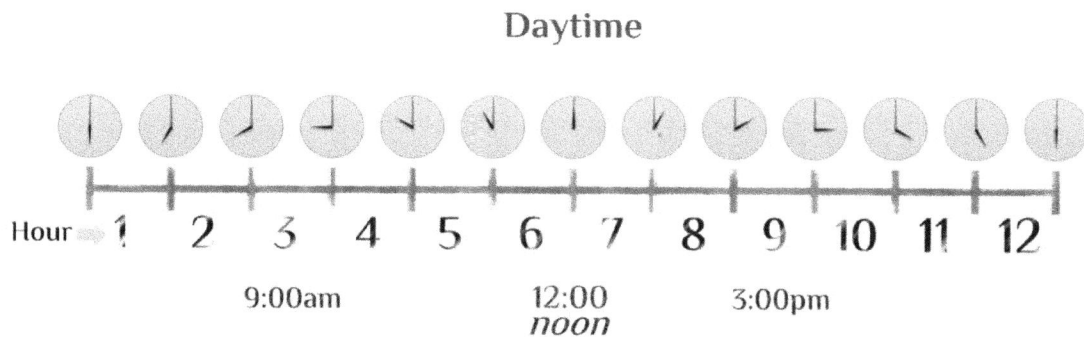

| Hour → | 1 | 2 | 3 | 4 | 5 | 6 | 7 | 8 | 9 | 10 | 11 | 12 |

9:00am   12:00 *noon*   3:00pm

The following table compares modern times-of-day to the Biblical hours:

Biblical Hour	Approximate 24-Hour Clock	Approximate 12-hour Clock
First	6:00-7:00	6:00am – 7:00am
Second	7:00-8:00	7:00am – 8:00am
Third	8:00-9:00	8:00am – 9:00am
Fourth	9:00-10:00	9:00am – 10:00am
Fifth	10:00-11:00	10:00am – 11:00am
Sixth	11:00-12:00	11:00am – 12:00pm
Seventh	12:00-13:00	12:00pm – 1:00pm
Eighth	13:00-14:00	1:00pm – 2:00pm
Ninth	14:00-15:00	2:00pm – 3:00pm
Tenth	15:00-16:00	3:00pm – 4:00pm
Eleventh	16:00-17:00	4:00pm – 5:00pm
Twelfth	17:00-18:00	5:00pm – 6:00pm

You may be thinking that the length of an hour would be dependent on the time of year and the latitude of the country, and you would be correct. The summertime hours in Israel, for example, are very long when compared to its wintertime hours since the duration of daylight in June is several hours longer than the duration of daylight in December. Because of this, the duration of an hour in June is relatively long when compared to an hour in the winter. The hours were probably tracked by shadows on some type of sundial.

To see a practical application of biblical hours, I recommend that you read Jesus' parable of the *Laborers in the Vineyard* (Matthew 20:1–16). In addition to mentioning "early in the morning," Jesus refers to the third, sixth, ninth, and eleventh hours, which are important for understanding the point of the parable.

Other examples of biblical hours have been provided below:

- While Jesus was on the cross, darkness fell over the land from the sixth hour to the ninth hour. Matthew 27:45

- Jesus invited two of John's disciples at the tenth hour. John 1:39

- Jesus encountered the Samaritan woman at Jacob's well at the sixth hour. John 4:6

- On the day of Pentecost, the apostles addressed the crowds in their own languages at the third hour. Acts 2:15

- Cornelius recounted that during the sixth hour, a man stood before him in shining garments. Acts 10:9

Twilight

Twilight is an important timing concept when studying the Appointed Times. Moses gave the following instructions about the Passover lamb to the people:

*"You shall keep it until the fourteenth day of the same month, then the whole assembly of the congregation of Israel is to kill it at **twilight**."*

Exodus 12:6 (Emphasis added)

Twilight- Literally "Between the Two Evenings" (Exodus 12:6)

In the above passage, twilight literally means **between the two evenings**. In our modern world, twilight refers to the time after the sun has set, while the sky is still illuminated with soft, diffused light. Twilight can also refer to the morning twilight, which occurs before the sun rises and the atmosphere is illuminated with the soft, diffused light of the sun.

For lack of a better term, many modern Bible translations use the term "twilight" to translate Moses' words *between the two evenings*, while some translations simply refer to it as "evening." It is interesting that Moses was the only biblical writer who used this phrase; it is found in Exodus, Leviticus, and Numbers.

The obvious question, of course, is what are the two evenings? It seems strange that the issue has not been settled, especially since scholars have been wrestling with it for almost 3,500 years. The question has puzzled students of God's Word for thousands of years. So, for your benefit, I will list the four most popular views and then explain which I believe is the most likely option.

Tracking Time in Israel

Four Views of "between the two evenings"

1. **Between sundown and complete darkness**

   » It is unlikely that this view is valid, because it would actually be the next day if the sun had already set. This is important in the case of Passover, since the people were required to sacrifice the Passover lamb on the 14th. If the sun had already set, then the date would have become the 15th, meaning they had missed their window for completing the task.

2. **Between sundown at the beginning of the day and sundown at the end of the day**

   » It is unlikely that this view is valid, because it would include the entire 24-hour day, so there is really no purpose in stipulating a time, since it could be anytime of the day.

3. **The time between noon and sundown**

   » This view holds some possibility since the beginning of the first evening can be determined by increasing shadow length due to the declining sun.

4. **Between the time of the evening sacrifice and sundown.** The evening sacrifice was offered at the 9th hour, which is 3:00pm by our modern timing. The people would have sacrificed the Passover lamb between 3:00pm and sundown.

   » This view is the most plausible for several reasons that are explained below.

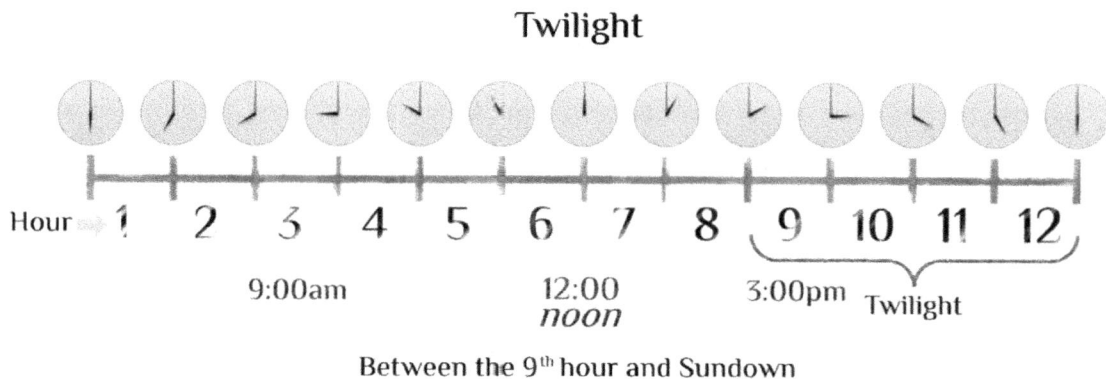

Twilight

Hour 1 2 3 4 5 6 7 8 9 10 11 12

9:00am   12:00   3:00pm Twilight
                noon

Between the 9th hour and Sundown

15

Twilight – Between the 9th Hour and Sundown

As we try to understand the meaning of *two evenings*, we can safely assume that the second of the two evenings is the end of the day, which is indicated by sundown. So, now the question is **what is the first evening?** The 29th chapter of Exodus holds some interesting clues that relate to this mystery. Let's look into this chapter to see what we can learn.

In Exodus 29:38–42, Moses explains the Lord's command to offer a one-year-old male lamb in the morning and *evening* of each day as a continual burnt offering throughout all of Israel's generations. In this passage, he uses the same phrase, "between the two evenings." So, we can infer that this daily offering is presented in the morning and later in the day, which is called *evening*. As history revealed, the Jewish community interpreted the timing of the sacrifice to be soon after sunrise and, in a similar way, the evening sacrifice was offered shortly before sunset.

With a little more investigation, we find that the Jewish priests, during the second temple period[5], were committed to offering the evening sacrifice **at the ninth hour of each day**, even if it resulted in their own physical harm or death. Josephus, the first-century historian, recorded how the Jewish priests faithfully continued their temple service even during the Roman siege of Jerusalem. Josephus related the following account of the situation:

"[A]nyone may hence learn how very great piety we exercise towards God, and the observance of his laws, since the priests were not at all hindered from their sacred ministrations, by their fear during this siege, but did still twice each day, in the morning and about the ninth hour, offer their sacrifices on the altar; nor did they omit those sacrifices, if any melancholy

---

5   *The second temple period began in 597 BC and ended in 70 AD, when the Romans destroyed the temple.*

accident happened, by the stones that were thrown among them. "[6]

From Josephus' record, we learn that the Jewish priests in the first century understood that *between the two evenings* meant to **begin at the ninth hour (3:00pm)**.

The between the two evenings concept gives some latitude in the timing of the priestly responsibilities, since the sacrifice could legitimately be offered anytime between the ninth hour and sundown. So for our understanding, we will consider *twilight* or *between the two evenings* as the time period between the ninth hour and the end-of-day, which is at sunset.

Twilight or Between the Two Evenings

Begins at the ninth hour of the day (3:00pm)

and

Ends at sunset

---

6   *(Josephus 1994) The Antiquities of the Jews, Book 14, Chapter 4, 3 (65) (Emphasis added).*

Nighttime

In the ancient world, nighttime was divided into **four equal parts**, beginning at sunset and ending at sunrise. Each part was called a *watch*, not like the watch that we wear on our wrists, but referring to guards *watching* over the city.

Nighttime was divided into four equal parts, beginning at sundown and ending at sunrise.

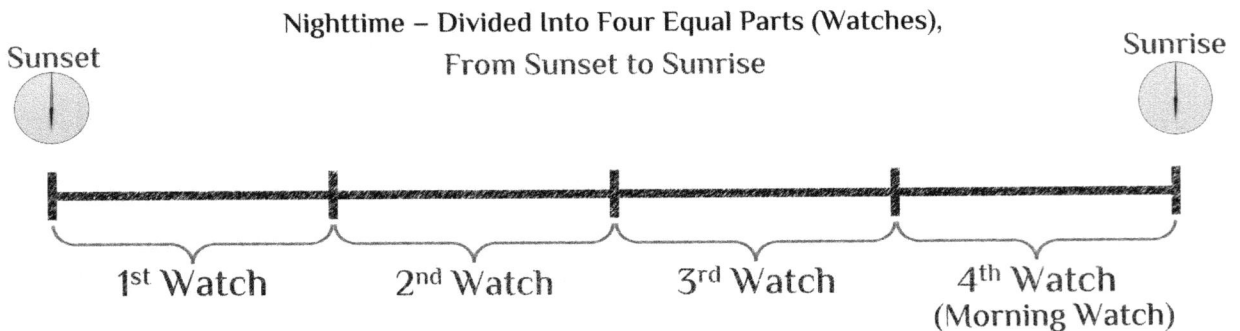

Nighttime – Divided Into Four Equal Parts (Watches), From Sunset to Sunrise

Sunset

Sunrise

1st Watch   2nd Watch   3rd Watch   4th Watch (Morning Watch)

The first watch began at sunset and continued for approximately one fourth of the nighttime; it was followed by the second, third, and finally by the fourth watch. The fourth watch was sometimes called the *morning* watch, since the watchmen literally watched for the rising of the sun, which ended their shift. The shifts may have been timed with sand-clocks or water-clocks, but little is known about how the ancients tracked time during the hours of darkness.

The Scriptures mention the watches of the night in various ways. Consider the following verses to see if they make more sense to you now:

Tracking Time in Israel

For a thousand years in Your sight
Are like yesterday when it passes by,
*Or **as a watch in the night**.*

Psalm 90:4 (Emphasis added)

*At the **morning watch**, the LORD looked down on the army of the Egyptians through the pillar of fire and cloud and brought the army of the Egyptians into confusion.*

Exodus 14:24 (Emphasis added)

When I remember You on my bed,
*I meditate on You **in the night watches**,*

Psalm 63:6 (Emphasis added)

*My eyes anticipate **the night watches**,*
That I may meditate on Your word.

Psalm 119:148 (Emphasis added)

*And in **the fourth watch** of the night He came to them, walking on the sea.*

Matthew 14:25 (Emphasis added)

Whether he comes in the second watch, or even in the third,
and finds them so, blessed are those slaves.

Luke 12:38 (Emphasis added)

Other passages include: Judges 7:19, 1 Samuel 11:11, 1 Chronicles 9:27, and Psalm 130:6.

Note: There is some evidence that only three watches were used during certain periods of Israel's history, but the concept of dividing the nighttime hours into equal segments or watches remains the same.

Midnight

Midnight is another important timing element that we find in the story of Israel's exodus from Egypt. The Hebrew word for midnight means half or mid. Since the ancients were not able to precisely track hours and minutes during darkness, they estimated the halfway point of the night, although it was probably not exactly at 12:00 midnight as it is defined in our modern world.

Week

Our modern world's concept of the seven-day week probably originated from ancient Israel's unbending commitment to observing the Sabbath on the seventh day of every week. Other civilizations had the concept of a seven-day week, but their weeks were not consistently seven days long. The ancient Babylonian calendar, for example, implemented a seven-day week by dividing the 29.5-day lunar month into four segments of seven days. But since the lunar month is slightly longer than 28 days, the fourth week of their month had to be stretched from seven days to eight.

It was not so with the Jewish people. For them, the Sabbath day occurred every seventh day, and the day after the Sabbath was always the first day of the next week. Thus, the word sabbath was sometimes used to refer to a seven-day period of time,[7] which we would call a week. The fact that a week could overlap from one month into the next was not an issue for them just as it is not an issue in our modern world.

---

7 *Leviticus 23:15 provides an example of the word sabbath referring to a period of seven days, or one week: "You shall also count for yourselves from the day after the sabbath, from the day when you brought in the sheaf of the wave offering; there shall be seven complete sabbaths." Also, Leviticus 25:8 uses sabbath synonymously with seven, but in this case it refers to seven years.*

The Hebrew language has a word for week, but it does not necessarily mean seven *days*; it refers to a *set of seven*, such as seven years or seven of anything.

The Sabbath Day

He ceased from His labor and was refreshed...

"Remember the Sabbath day, to keep it holy.
Six days you shall labor, and do all your work,
but the seventh day is a Sabbath to the Lord your God.

...

For in six days the Lord made heaven and earth,
the sea, and all that is in them, and rested on the seventh day;
Therefore the Lord blessed the Sabbath day and made it holy.

Exodus 20:8-11

Sabbath is more than just a timing word. More importantly, it is the first Appointed Time that is mentioned in Leviticus 23,[8] indicating its importance in the sight of God and in the life of Israel. Once again, it is observed on the seventh day of every week, which is Saturday. Based on what we have learned about days, the Sabbath begins at sundown on the sixth day and ends at sundown on the seventh day. Or stated differently, the Sabbath begins at sundown on Friday and ends at sundown on Saturday evening. Since the Sabbath occurs on the seventh day of every week, we sometimes refer to it as the weekly Sabbath in order to avoid confusion with great or high Sabbaths, which we will explore in a later section.

The Sabbath is the commemoration of the Lord's rest from His work after completing the six days of creation[9] and is intended to be a day of rest for everyone. The Hebrew word for Sabbath is *shabbat* and is based on the Hebrew word that means "and He rested," *shabath*, referring to God resting after His work of creation.[10] Resting from our labors is the essence of the Sabbath. It was given as a blessing from God so we can be refreshed

---

8 *Leviticus 23:2–3*

9 *Exodus 20:11 – "For in six days the Lord made the heavens and the earth, the sea and all that is in them, and rested on the seventh day; therefore the Lord blessed the sabbath day and made it holy."*

10 *Genesis 2:2 – "By the seventh day God completed His work which He had done, and He rested on the seventh day from all His work which He had done."*

as He was refreshed when He ceased from His labor.[11]

The Sabbath day was not just a commemoration. It is one of the hallmarks of God's covenant with Israel, to the extent that they would forever be known as God's people through their keeping the commandments regarding the Sabbath.[12]   Every Israelite is required to rest on the weekly Sabbath, including the head of the household, the entire family, the slaves/ servants, guests, and even the animals that belong to the household. The penalty for failing to keep the Sabbath was extremely severe, so the entire nation dutifully obeyed this command.

If someone were to ask you, "Which day is the Sabbath?" how would you respond? The Israelites observe the Sabbath as the seventh day of the week, which is Saturday.

"If because of the sabbath, you turn your foot
From doing your own pleasure on My holy day,
And call the sabbath a delight, the holy day of the Lord honorable,
And honor it, desisting from your own ways,
From seeking your own pleasure
And speaking your own word,

Then you will take delight in the Lord,
And I will make you ride on the heights of the earth;
And I will feed you with the heritage of Jacob your father,
For the mouth of the Lord has spoken."

Isaiah 58:13–14

---

11   *Exodus 31:17 – "It is a sign between Me and the sons of Israel forever; for in six days the Lord made heaven and earth, but on the seventh day He ceased from labor, and was refreshed."*
12   *Exodus 31:16–17a – "So the sons of Israel shall observe the sabbath, to celebrate the sabbath throughout their generations as a perpetual covenant. It is a sign between Me and the sons of Israel forever..."*

The origin of the Sabbath rest is very interesting. The Scriptures taught it as the way of the Lord even before the He gave His Law to Moses (see Exodus 16:22–30). According to the creation accounts in Genesis chapters 1 and 2, God rested on the seventh day, and even though the accounts do not contain an explicit command for mankind to rest, they offer a subtle, refreshing appeal for us to rest after our labors. What does your day of rest look like?

The Day of Preparation

The day *before* a Sabbath Day is referred to as *a day of preparation*. Shopping, chores, and laborious activities were completed on the day of preparation since work was forbidden on the Sabbath. Meals were prepared and clothes were cleaned and pressed in advance of the seventh day to assure that everyone could rest from their work on the Sabbath.

This is also the case with great or high Sabbaths, which are addressed in a later section. For example, the 14th day of Abib (the first month of the Hebrew religious calendar) is Passover and is also referred to as *the day of preparation* for the first high Sabbath, which is the Feast of Unleavened Bread on the 15th day of Abib. Preparation for this high Sabbath may be done on the 14th, but not on the 15th, since it is a high Sabbath, a day of rest.

A Sabbath Day's Journey

All travel had to be completed before the sun went down on a day of preparation, whether it was a journey to visit the sick or commuting to and from work. Riding an animal instead of walking did not release a person from the requirement for rest since forcing the animal to work as a beast of burden also violated the Sabbath.[13] Simply stated, God forbade all labor for both animals and humans on Sabbath Days.

The Talmud[14] places a limit on the maximum distance a person can travel on foot on the Sabbath day[15] — anything beyond that distance is considered to be labor and a violation of the Sabbath. This maximum distance is referred to as a *"Sabbath day's journey"* and was defined as 2,000 normal steps or 2,000 cubits, which is approximately 0.6 miles or 0.9 kilometers. It is interesting that the Talmud does not place a limit on how far a person could walk within a walled city.

Great or High Sabbaths

In addition to the weekly Sabbaths, **seven special Sabbaths were established by the Lord in His Appointed Times in Leviticus 23**. We refer to these Sabbaths as great or high Sabbaths, but for convenience we will simply refer to them as *high* Sabbaths.

The *high* Sabbath terminology is not common in the Scriptures, but it is certainly there. John 19:31, for example, refers to the first day of the Feast of Unleavened Bread as a high Sabbath, thus differentiating it from

---

13   Deuteronomy 5:12–14

14   The Talmud is the compilation of the Jewish oral laws that were recorded in written form after the destruction of the Temple in A.D. 70. The purpose of the Talmud was to provide information about how the laws and commands of Moses were to be carried out. Although it is not considered to be inspired, the Talmud provides extremely valuable insights about how Judaism was lived out through the centuries.

15   (Rodkinson, The Babylonian Talmud 1916) Book 4, TRACT BETZAH, Chapter II, p. 31

a *weekly* Sabbath. The underlying Greek word is *megas* (μέγας), from which we get the prefix *meg* or *mega*. Even in our modern world, when something is said to be mega, you know it's big or special. The term carries multiple meanings, all of which suggest something of great magnitude or magnificence.

Why would the Lord require a day of rest as part of His Appointed Times? Simply stated, I believe it is a way of telling us to honor the Lord by stopping, pausing, and considering what is being taught by this Appointed Time. We will explore the timing and substance of each high Sabbath in detail in our book *The Messiah Beyond a Shadow of Doubt*.

The seven high Sabbaths are listed in their annual order in the following table:

The Seven High Sabbaths

Easy! {

1   1st Day of Unleavened Bread – 15th day of 1st moon

2   7th Day of Unleavened Bread – 21st day of 1st moon

3   Feast of Weeks (50 Days after First Fruits)

4   Day of Trumpets – 1st day of 7th moon

5   Day of Atonement – 10th day of 7th moon

Easy! {

6   1st Day of Feast of Booths – 15th day of 7th moon

7   8th Day after the Feast of Booths begins – 22nd day of 7th moon

Since the high Sabbaths are found throughout the Scriptures, it would be worth your time to memorize them – it's really quite simple! Just remember that the first and last Appointed Times in Leviticus 23 are week-long feasts, and both begin and end with a high Sabbath— that makes it **Easy!** to remember. So, you now already know four of the seven high Sabbath Days, which makes it easier to memorize the remaining three high Sabbaths that occur in between them.

Notice that Passover is not listed in the table above because it is not a high Sabbath. As we've already discussed, Passover, which is always on Abib 14, is a day of preparation, or more specifically, the day of preparation for the first high Sabbath Day of the Feast of Unleavened Bread. It is a day of preparation because the Israelites prepare for the next day, Abib 15, which is the first day of the Feast of Unleavened Bread.

A word of caution: The terminology may be a little confusing at times. Even though Abib 14 is the date of the Lord's Passover,[16] the actual "pass over" event did not occur until midnight of Abib 15, when the destroyer *passed* over the homes that had the blood of the lamb on the doorposts and lintel.[17] We must also be careful as we study, because the Scriptures sometimes use the terms *Passover* and *The Feast of Unleavened Bread* interchangeably. Furthermore, the day before a *weekly* Sabbath is also called a day of preparation, so, it is important to give close attention to the context of a passage in order to know which type of Sabbath is being discussed.

High Sabbaths Occur Throughout the Scriptures

As you read through the Bible, you will begin to recognize the Appointed Times as they are mentioned, but they are sometimes

---

16   Leviticus 23:5 – *"In the first month, on the fourteenth day of the month at twilight is the Lord's Passover."*
17   Exodus 12:23b – *"...the Lord will pass over the door and will not allow the destroyer to come in to your houses to smite you."*

mentioned by their dates, rather than by their names so, knowing their dates and the names will add color and precision to your understanding of the Bible.

Month

When the Lord conveyed His Appointed Times to Moses, He was very specific about the months in which they were to be observed. The spring Appointed Times begin in the month of Abib, the first month of the year, while the *fall* Appointed Times are observed during the month of Tishri, which is the seventh month of the year. In the following figure, the months of the Hebrew calendar are positioned next to the more familiar months of the Gregorian calendar[18]   to help you visualize how the calendars relate to each other.

Comparison of the Gregorian and Hebrew Months

(Alternate names are in parentheses)

Gregorian	Hebrew
January	
	Sh'vat
February	
	Adar
March	
	Abib (Nisan)
April	
	Iyar (Zif)
May	
	Sivan
June	
	Tammuz
July	
	Av
August	
	Elul
September	
	Tishri (Ethaninm)
October	
	Cheshvan (Bul)
November	
	Kislev
December	
	Tevet

---

18   *The Gregorian calendar is the most widely used calendar in the world. It was implemented by Pope Gregory XIII in October of 1582. Before that time, the Julian calendar was in use in the western world since 46 BC, but due to its inaccuracies, the dates for the holy days had become unreliable.*

Notice that the months of the Hebrew calendar seem to occur in-between the months of the Gregorian calendar. Passover and the resurrection of Christ, for example, are always observed in the March-April timeframe of the Gregorian calendar, since the Scriptures teach that they occurred during the Hebrew month of Abib. Likewise, the Day of Atonement is always observed in the September-October timeframe during the Hebrew month of Tishri.

The months of the Gregorian calendar will always occur during the same seasons of the year since they are based on earth's position as it revolves around the sun. The Hebrew months, on the other hand, do not begin on a fixed day of the solar year, which is the reason the dates of the Appointed Times shift from year to year on the Gregorian calendar. The Hebrew months begin on varying dates of the solar year since they are determined by the phases of the moon, which are not in sync with the solar year.

The duration of a lunar month is 29 days, 12 hours, and 44 minutes[19], which is roughly 29.5 days. That means that, after 12 lunar months, there are about 11 days remaining in the solar year.[20] Because of this, the Hebrew months will not occur on the same Gregorian dates from year to year — they would occur approximately 11 days earlier in the following year if an adjustment is not made.

---

19   *Based on the synodic month*
20   *29.5 days x 12 months = 354 days, which is 11 days less than the 365 days of the solar*

Does the Hebrew Year Always Contain Twelve Months?

Since the solar and lunar years differ in length, a special intercalary month,[21] called **Adar** II, is inserted into the Hebrew calendar immediately *before* the month of Adar during certain years. If this correction is not made, then the Appointed Times and other events on the calendar would occur at different seasons each year. For example, it would be possible that Passover could occur in the fall or in the summer, or any other time of the year, rather than during the early spring months, as did the first Passover during the exodus from Egypt. Without the adjustment of the intercalary month, the required grain offerings would not be available for the people since the dates of their worship might not coincide with the timing of their harvests.

Because of this additional intercalary month, some years on the Hebrew calendar contain 13 months. The intercalary month is a concept that is similar to the leap year in the Gregorian calendar, which inserts an extra day in February every four years. This technique assures that the spring Appointed Times will always occur in the springtime, rather than sliding throughout the seasons of the solar year. Likewise, it assures that the fall Appointed Times will always be in the autumn, in the September-October timeframe.

The intercalary month is not randomly inserted into the Hebrew calendar. It is inserted in specific years that are predetermined by a lunar-solar cycle that is known as the Metonic Cycle. The Metonic Cycle repeats every 19 years and identifies years 3, 6, 8, 11, 14, 17, and 19 as years that must have an additional month in order to synchronize the Hebrew calendar with the solar seasons. You can research the Metonic Cycle to learn more about this phenomenon.

---

21 *Intercalary month refers to an additional month that is added to the year during certain years. It is similar to an additional day (i.e., February 29th) that is added to the Gregorian calendar during a leap year.*

New Moon, New Month

The Hebrew months begin with the appearance of the new moon. The Jewish leaders, therefore, carefully tracked the moon throughout its various phases. Even though they were able to calculate the date of the new moon, their rule was to rely on the testimony of witnesses who actually observed it.

Jewish New Moon
Courtesy of Nasa

Witnesses were examined by the Council in a large court in Jerusalem called Beth Ya'azeq. Once the Council was satisfied that the witnesses' testimonies were true, they would then consecrate the new moon and proclaim throughout the land that a new month had begun.[22]

The methods of proclaiming the new moon varied throughout Israel's history. In Numbers 10:1–2, the Lord instructed Moses to "Make yourself two trumpets of silver, of hammered work." The trumpets were designated for multiple uses, but in verse 10, we are told that they should also be used to proclaim the first days of the months.

---

22   (Rodkinson, The Babylonian Talmud 1916) Book 2, TRACT ROSH HASHANA, FESTIVALS PART 1, "NEW YEAR" – Chapter II, p. 45-46

*"Also in the day of your gladness and in your appointed feasts,
and on the first days of your months…"*

Numbers 10:10

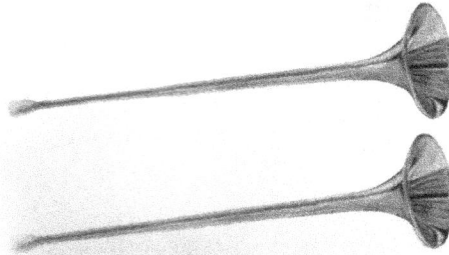

Trumpets were eventually replaced by the lighting of signal bonfires[23] and later by sending messengers throughout the land.

---

23   (Rodkinson, The Babylonian Talmud 1916) Book 2, TRACT ROSH HASHANA, FESTIVALS PART 1, "NEW YEAR" – Chapter II, p. 42

The Silver-Edge Moon - A New Month

What does a Jewish new moon look like? Although the Israelites could have chosen any phase of the moon to indicate a new month, they chose the phase when the illumination from the sun begins to appear on the edge of the moon. This phase is informally known as the Silver Edge moon, shown in the left-hand side of Figure 23.[24] You should know that the phase when the moon has no illumination, and is completely dark, is also called a new moon, but it is the astronomical new moon shown in the right-hand side of Figure 23. The astronomical new moon is used by modern astronomers, but it is not the same as the Jewish new moon – be careful not to confuse them!

The Silver Edge – 1st Day The Jewish New Moon

– A new month has begun! –

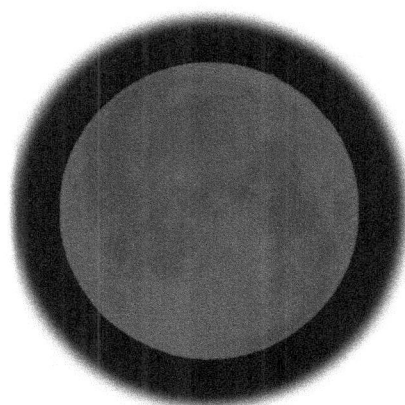

Astronomical New Moon A new month will soon be here!

Figure 23

Remember, an astronomical new moon does not signal a new month in Judaism—the new month is signaled only by the appearance of the new silver edge moon.

---

24   *The moon phases that are pictured are from the northern hemisphere. Moon phases in the southern hemisphere appear to be the opposite or mirror image, since the north and the south view the moon upside-down from each other.*

The Phases of the Moon

You may be wondering what causes the moon's phases. Having a basic understanding of the phases of the moon will give insight into the approximate day of the month of the lunar calendar, when the Appointed Times begin and end, and whether we are in the first or latter half of the current month.

With the exception of an eclipse, half of the moon is always illuminated by the sun, but from our perspective on earth, we are only able to see a portion of that illumination. When the earth is directly between the sun and the moon, the moon appears to be fully illuminated, but as the moon circles around the earth in its 29 ½ day orbit, we are not able to see the fully illuminated hemisphere—we can only see a portion of it until it becomes like a narrow sliver. When the moon is directly between the earth and the sun, we are unable to see any of its illuminated hemisphere, and it appears to be completely dark. This is the reason for the astronomical new moon, which is shown in the lower right-hand corner of the image below.

Moon Phases

The Moon Phases image shows some of the phases of the moon that appear after the silver edge new moon. The Hebrew month, of course, begins when the silver edge (*upper left-hand corner of the Moon Phases image*) occurs after the astronomical new moon (*pictured in the lower right-hand corner of the Moon Phases image*).

At times, the moon seems to be so close that you might think you could hit it with a stone. But it is actually much farther than it appears. The following is a scale image of the relative size of the earth, the moon, and the distance between them, which averages 238,900 miles or 384,472 kilometers.

238,855 miles

Year

If someone were to ask, "When does the Jewish year begin?" the correct response would be, "Which year do you mean?" You may have heard that the Jewish new year is observed on Rosh Hashana, which falls on Tishri 1 in the September-October timeframe. But, just before the exodus from Egypt, the Lord told Moses and Aaron that Abib (aka. Aviv or Nisan) shall be the beginning of months,[25] which falls during the March-April timeframe. Both of these dates mark the beginning of years on the Jewish calendar. Rosh Hashana, which means head of the year, marks the beginning of the civil year, while the first day of Abib marks the beginning of the year for religious observances. Jewish law also has two additional dates which mark the beginning of years, meaning that Judaism has four new year observances.

---

25   *Exodus 13:4, 23:15, 34:18 and Deuteronomy 16:1*

According to the Talmud,[26]

> *"The first of Abib or Nisan is the new* **year for kings and for festivals, which includes the Appointed Times.**
>
> *The first of Elul is the new year* **for the tithing of animals.**
>
> *The first of Tishri is the new year* **for years, which included Sabbatical years, Jubilee years, and for the planting and for vegetables.**
>
> *The first of Shevat is the new year* **for trees** *(Note: The House of Hillel considers the fifteenth of Shevat to be the new year for trees)."*

The additional years can be likened to fiscal years or academic years, which provide a convenience for accounting and school activities. Josephus, the first-century Jewish historian, wrote that Tishri 1 was actually the original new-year date for buying and selling, so Moses preserved that as the original order of the months. But Moses said that Nisan (i.e., Abib) should be the first month for their festivals because God brought them out of Egypt in that month. "So that this month began the year as to all the solemnities they observed to honor God."[27]

---

26 *(Rodkinson, The Babylonian Talmud 1916) Book 2, TRACT ROSH HASHANA, FESTIVALS PART 1, "NEW YEAR" – Chapter I, p1: "MISHNA I.: There are four New Year days, viz.: The first of Nissan is New Year for (the ascension of) Kings and for (the regular rotation of) festivals; the first of Elul is New Year for the cattle-tithe, but according to R. Eliezer and R. Simeon, it is on the first of Tishri. The first of Tishri is New Year's day, for ordinary years, and for sabbatic years and jubilees; and also for the planting of trees and for herbs. On the first day of Shebhat is the New Year for trees, according to the school of Shammai; but the school of Hillel says it is on the fifteenth of the same month."*

27 *(Josephus 1994) The Antiquities of the Jews, Book 1, Chapter 3, 3 (81)*

When does the month of Abib begin? As a general rule of thumb,[28] it begins when the first new moon (i.e., the silver edge) is observed that occurs after the spring equinox (in the northern hemisphere[29]). Two equinoxes occur during each solar year—one in the spring (i.e., the vernal equinox) and one in the fall (i.e., the autumnal equinox). The word equinox is derived from a Latin term that means equal night, referring to specific days during the solar year when the amount of daylight is almost the same as the amount of darkness.

The Original Meaning of Abib

The Hebrew word "Abib" originally referred to green ears of grain, rather than to a month. It was synonymous with springtime.   Thus, the lunar month in which the barley ears were green but not fully ripe for harvest became known as the month of Abib. The first fruits offering of Leviticus 23:9–14 consisted of a sheaf of barley that was abib—that is, the grain had matured to a head, but it was still green and not fully ripe. Using this original meaning of abib, the start of a year could have been delayed for a month in the event of a long winter.

Regardless of how the month of Abib was determined, it was the first month of the year for religious observances. But the Hebrew calendar was later refined so that the new year, beginning with Abib, was based on soli-lunar (i.e., sun and moon) events that are described by the Metonic cycle. After the Babylonian exile, the month of Abib became known as Nisan, so the two names are synonymous.

---

28   *This is a general rule of thumb, but you should be aware that many variables factor into the determination of the beginning of months and years. The eastern and western churches use different criteria for determining these dates.*

29   *Although the equinox occurs on the same day in the northern and southern hemispheres, the names are different, since the beginning of springtime in the northern hemisphere is the beginning of autumn in the southern hemisphere. Thus, the month of Abib is based on the vernal equinox in the northern hemisphere.*

Summary

You will find that having an understanding of the ancient Hebrew calendaring system can reveal insights into how the Appointed Times and various events of the Scriptures fit together. But you will also find that having this knowledge will unlock clues that can explain other parts of the Scriptures, as well. I hope this information will become second nature to you, so you will not have to refer to this guide. But until then, may it be a valuable resource for you as you study the Bible.

Bibliography

Josephus, F. (1994). *The Works of Josephus*. (W. Whiston, Trans.) Peabody, Massachusets, USA: Hendrickson Publishers, Inc.

Rodkinson, M. L. (1903). *The Babylonian Talmud* (English Edition ed.). (M. L. Rodkinson, Ed., & M. L. Rodkinson, Trans.) New York: New Talmud Publishing Society.

Rodkinson, M. L. (1916). *The Babylonian Talmud* (Vol. 2). Boston, USA: New Talmud Publishing Society.

www.ingramcontent.com/pod-product-compliance
Lightning Source LLC
Chambersburg PA
CBHW081652270326
41933CB00018B/3444